IMAGES
of America

MOUNT AIRY

Mount Airy was the name William Allen gave in 1750 to his country estate on high ground now occupied by the Lutheran Theological Seminary. Since 1807, several schools have occupied this site. In 1826, Col. Augustus Roumfort, trained at West Point, founded the American Classical and Military Lyceum. Fights between town boys, called "Rips," and college boys were common. Future generals George Meade (Union) and Pierre Beauregard (Confederate) were students. James Gowen demolished the old Mount Airy house about 1848 and built Magnolia Villa. (The Library Company of Philadelphia.)

On the cover: In 1887, artist and photographer George Bacon Wood photographed sheep going to market, with his house at 6708 Germantown Avenue in the background. Until seven years before this photograph was taken, tolls were charged on this Germantown and Perkiomen Turnpike. In 1801, it cost 6¢ for 20 sheep to be driven on the road. The trolley tracks curving off to the right enter the passenger railway depot, still there today. (The Library Company of Philadelphia.)

IMAGES
of America

MOUNT AIRY

Elizabeth Farmer Jarvis

ARCADIA
PUBLISHING

Published by Arcadia Publishing
Charleston, South Carolina

Library of Congress Catalog Card Number: 2007937759

For all general information contact Arcadia Publishing at:
Telephone 843-853-2070
Fax 843-853-0044
E-mail sales@arcadiapublishing.com
For customer service and orders:
Toll-Free 1-888-313-2665

Visit us on the Internet at www.arcadiapublishing.com

A photographer captured this scene from an upper window at Engard's Bakery (see page 70), looking up Germantown Avenue toward East Mount Airy Avenue, about 1905. The top of the Schaeffer-Ashmead Memorial Church of the Lutheran Theological Seminary is visible in the distance. The porches of the White Swan Hotel are on the left. The two residences on the right are gone, as is the milestone beside the curb in the center of the photograph. (P. J. McMenamin.)

CONTENTS

ACKNOWLEDGMENTS

A generous financial contribution from Richard Wood Snowden made this book possible. I am also grateful for the contributions of Sandy Drinker, Dan Muroff, Janet Potter, Elise Rivers, Thekla Scott, Meredith Sonderskov, and in memory of Eversley S. Vaughan, Samuel F. Long, and Mark Gilbert. David Young, executive director of Cliveden of the National Trust, and Michael Kleiner, president of the Mount Airy Business Association helped enlist financial support from Apple Roofing; Doris Belson, psychotherapist; Classic Management; Greenhouse Internists; Macintosh Construction Company; MacLens Collision Repair; Mt. Airy Custom Furniture; and Weavers Way Co-Op Market.

All the photographs in this book are from the Germantown Historical Society (GHS) unless otherwise credited. Judith Callard and Irvin Miller of the society were tremendous supporters, helping me uncover many resources at the GHS library and sharing their vast storehouse of Mount Airy information. J. M. Duffin amazed me with his comprehensive knowledge of Mount Airy history, often having the most minute details in his head. I thank David T. Moore for sharing his collection and knowledge of local history. Lois Frischling contributed her expertise and collection of Pelham items. Judith, Jim, David, and Lois read the manuscript to ensure accuracy. I am indebted to scholars David Contosta and Jefferson M. Moak for allowing me to build on their research. Elise Rivers did some fine sleuthing to identify houses. Andrew Maginnis provided his train and trolley expertise, and Joseph B. Van Sciver III advised on automobiles. David Kerper and Marc McCarron of Kerper Studio tackled many photography challenges. Susan Schindler contributed her editing skills. Erin Vosgien, Arcadia's fine editor, was cheerful and quick to respond.

I am indebted to Meredith Sonderskov and George Bryant for their hours of work on promotion and fund-raising, and to Veronica Aplenc, the executive director of the Chestnut Hill Historical Society, for her support.

Thanks to all who contributed photographs or information: African American Museum in Philadelphia; Allens Lane Art Center; Atwater Kent Museum; Awbury Arboretum; Cynthia Best; Judith Callard; Chestnut Hill Historical Society; Dena Dannenberg; Andrew Domanski; J. M. Duffin; Fairmount Park Commission; Debbie Feldman; the Forbes Collection, New York (all rights reserved); Free Library of Philadelphia; Germantown Jewish Centre; Lilinau V. Goffney; Grace Epiphany Church; Louetta Ray Hadley; Historical Society of Pennsylvania; Sally Melcher Jarvis; Victoria Koursaros; The Library Company of Philadelphia; Livezey family; Lovett Memorial Library; Lutheran Archives Center at Philadelphia; McCoubrey/Overholser Building Construction; P. J. McMenamin; Andrew Maginnis; Antje Mattheus and David Kairys; David T. Moore; Mount Airy Presbyterian Church; Don Murphy; Pennsylvania School for the Deaf; Philadelphia City Archives; Carol A. Hall Mack; Project Learn School; Tom Rebbie, Philadelphia Toboggan Coasters Corporation; the Rothe family; St. Madeleine Sophie Church; Sedgwick Cultural Center; Philip Seitz; Laura Siena; Temple University Libraries, Urban Archives; Richard Wood Snowden; and Ted Xaras.

Special thanks to Andrew, Judy, Anne, and Alex Jarvis for always being there for me.

INTRODUCTION

Mount Airy was the name William Allen gave in 1750 to his 47-acre country estate on the high ground now occupied by the Lutheran Theological Seminary. Mount Airy eventually became the name of the surrounding neighborhood. Allen, chief justice of Pennsylvania and one of the wealthiest men in the colony, was a partner in a Philadelphia mercantile firm for 50 years. One of the firm's interests was dealing in slaves. When Allen's son James predeceased him in 1778, James's will stated, "My three negro Slaves Frances, Sampson & Harry, shall be henceforth free & manumitted, I having ever been persuaded of the injustice."

In 1689, the earliest settlers in this section of the Germantown Township (established in 1683) had built a small village, named Cresheim for their German homeland. By 1700, 12 houses had been built along Cresheim Road, then the area's main road. It ran from what is now Carpenter Lane to Kerper's Lane (currently Springfield Avenue in Chestnut Hill). Following the old Native American Minsi Path, Germantown Road also ran through the area in the 17th century, connecting Philadelphia with outlying towns. Much of present Mount Airy consists of the "Sidelands" lots of the Germantown Township, the area between the current Washington Lane and Sedgwick Street. These secondary lots were given to lot owners in Germantown village to ensure that they owned equal amounts of land. Mount Airy remained a rural area, with a thriving milling community along the Cresheim and Wissahickon Creeks, for much of the next two centuries.

In the first half of the 18th century, most Mount Airy residents practiced a trade and maintained a garden plot, chickens, and a cow. The tide of German settlers peaked in the mid-18th century. Most immigrants who arrived in the Germantown Township were skilled craftsmen: weavers, tanners, shoemakers, wagon makers, and other cottage industry workers.

On October 4, 1777, the Battle of Germantown brought the Revolutionary War to the village's doorsteps, as George Washington's troops attacked the British up and down the Germantown Road. The first skirmish was at Allens Lane. The Americans fired cannons at British forces barricaded in Benjamin Chew's stone mansion, Cliveden, but could not defeat them. Retreating, the Americans lost 152 men, and the British lost 70. Ordinary citizens endured many trials. Bullets whizzed by their houses, British troops marauded their property for supplies, and many helped bury the dead in the aftermath.

A stagecoach ran through Mount Airy between Philadelphia and Bethlehem as early as 1763. In 1812, one observer counted 500 wagons in one day on Germantown Avenue, many drawn by six or eight horses. From 1801 to 1870, Germantown Avenue was a toll road from Third and Vine Streets to where Collegeville is now. In 1870, the City of Philadelphia purchased the interests of the Germantown and Perkiomen Turnpike Company and closed the toll gates. In 1877, after years of neglect to the road's surface, Belgian block was laid as far as Gorgas Lane. The section from Gorgas to Bethlehem Pike was completed about three years later.

In the 18th century, the area between Washington Lane and Sedgwick Street was called Beggarstown. In the 19th century, an effort was made to rename the area Franklinville. Dogtown was yet another name for the area, supposedly named for the spotted dogs at the Franklinville Fire Company. The village of Mount Pleasant was located around Germantown and Mount Pleasant Avenues.

Many early Philadelphia city dwellers looked to the Germantown Township as a refuge or a summer retreat and later as a garden suburb. George W. Carpenter, Germantown native son of humble background, made a fortune in the drug business and real estate. In the 1840s, Carpenter amassed 350 acres and built a colossal Greek Revival mansion. Phil-Ellena was replaced by the fashionable development Pelham 50 years later.

The introduction of the railroad to Germantown in 1832, and then to Chestnut Hill through Mount Airy in 1854, made Mount Airy more accessible to the business district in downtown Philadelphia. In 1859, horses pulling passenger cars on rails went as far as Phil-Ellena Street. In 1884, the Pennsylvania Railroad opened the west line, causing more housing to be constructed. Factories sprang up along the railroad lines. Trolleys replaced horsecars between 1894 and 1896. Before then, workers at all economic levels had to live within walking or horse-riding distance of their work. These changes caused the Germantown Avenue spine of Mount Airy to fill in with commercial buildings where there had once been pastures, fields, and houses. A fresh grid of streets was created perpendicular to Germantown Avenue, sometimes causing the destruction of 18th-century houses on the avenue and supplanting the old estates and farms.

From 1844 to 1854, the borough of Germantown extended north to Washington Lane (originally called Abington Lane). The township of Germantown, including Mount Airy and Chestnut Hill, extended from there to Northwestern Avenue. In 1854, Philadelphia consolidated boroughs and townships into the county of Philadelphia, making this area part of the 22nd Ward.

Even after its consolidation into Philadelphia, much of Mount Airy remained a sparsely populated rural area as late as 1870. The east side of Mount Airy had few roads, except for what is now Gowen Avenue (Miller's or Wolf's Lane), Mount Airy Avenue, Gorgas Lane, and Church (later called Phil-Ellena), Sharpnack, Pleasant, and Chew Streets. A swamp, which fed the Wingohocking Creek, lay between what is now Chew Avenue and Boyer Street, around Mount Pleasant Avenue.

With its open land close to Philadelphia, Mount Airy became home to many institutions, such as the Pennsylvania School for the Deaf and the Lutheran Orphans' Home and Asylum for the Aged.

The boundaries of Mount Airy have changed over the years and are subject to interpretation. As late as the 1920s, Mount Airy's northern boundary was considered to be Mermaid Lane and its eastern boundary Cheltenham Avenue. In the 19th and early 20th century, the southern boundary was usually considered to be Gorgas and Carpenter Lanes; most residents south of these streets considered themselves to be from Germantown. Today the U.S. Postal Service defines the boundaries of Mount Airy by its zip code, 19119, which extends north to the Cresheim Creek, east to Stenton Avenue, south to Johnson Street, and west to the Wissahickon Creek. The political boundary to the west, however, is Wissahickon Avenue. The West Mt. Airy Neighbors and East Mt. Airy Neighbors organizations consider Washington Lane to be Mount Airy's southern edge.

In Mount Airy, row houses intermingled with single-family houses, allowing for mixed incomes. In the 20th century, Mount Airy became nationally known for the successful efforts of an interracial group to combat unfair practices against African Americans by some realtors. Hoping to cause white flight to the suburbs, these realtors would profit from the quick turnover of house sales. Around 1954, three religious institutions formed a council, pledging to build "acquaintance and understanding across group and color lines." Mount Airy became one of the few neighborhoods in America celebrated for its racial integration.

This book covers the history of Mount Airy from the time of European settlement to the 1960s. Today it is a diverse mixture of residences, businesses, and institutions. The people of Mount Airy celebrate its legacy of tolerance, diversity, activism, and history.

One

EARLY DEVELOPMENT

The date 1698 was marked in plaster on the gable end just below the roof of this house, built by Heivert Papen on the northwest corner of Germantown Avenue and Johnson Street across from Cliveden. The house passed into the Johnson family in the early 18th century and survived until 1883, when it was torn down to make way for Victorian twin houses.

Built in 1756, Philip Weaver's house at 6611 Germantown Avenue was rented for a parsonage by the Church of the Brethren, whose present-day church is just to the north. In the early 19th century, it was used as a school and, between 1893 and 1901, again as a parsonage. This house was demolished in 1907 to make way for the present parsonage. The roof is wood shingled, and the original stone walls were covered only on the front with scored stucco. Also on the site was this log and stone house (below), built in 1731 for Alexander Mack, the founder of the Brethren or "Dunkers." After his death, his son Johannes, a stocking weaver, lived there. Note the straw hat leaning on the fence to the right.

Reputedly built in 1700, this barn and house share a wall, a common style in Germany. The oldest section of the house was said to have red tiles from Germany on the roof. Pictured here in 1903, only part of the barn wall remains standing—the result of a fire in 1896. Note the pants hanging on the fence. The Unruh family owned this property between Chew Street (later Chew Avenue) and the Chestnut Hill Railroad, south of what is now Pleasant Street.

In the 1760s, Cornelius Cunrads probably built this house and barn at 7513 Germantown Avenue. Sebastian Miller sold it in 1782 to Peter Nace. Later William Lehman Schaeffer, who owned the property across the street that would later become Pennsylvania School for the Deaf, sold it in 1872 to Franklin B. Gowen, who continued to expand his family's land. In 1927, the house and barn were demolished, and row houses took their place. (Free Library of Philadelphia.)

The upper part of Mount Airy was first settled along Cresheim Road, not Germantown Avenue. Parts of Cresheim Road remain today, its course now altered by the railroad line around Allens Lane. Pictured in 1899, probably looking toward Chestnut Hill, this farmhouse with stalks of corn in the yard sits by Cresheim Road, north of Allens Lane, near the Cresheim Creek. Matthias Milan acquired 100 acres of land in Cresheim and built this house (below) around 1710 to 1720. It is photographed here around 1920 on Cresheim Road above Allens Lane. The rear of the Victorian-style houses on Rural Lane, developed by Henry H. Houston, are visible in the distance. It was owned by the Bolter family during the second half of the 19th century, then bought by Houston, and demolished in the 1920s. (Below, Historical Society of Pennsylvania.)

The Monastery house is all that remains of a former milling and manufacturing center that Joseph Gorgas built along the Wissahickon Creek around 1751. The Monastery was named for the log house that preceded it, built in 1737 by three Pietists, who called it the Kloster (cloister). Seventh-Day Baptists from the area met here until 1739, when the group split. Many moved to the Ephrata Cloister in Lancaster County, where Gorgas grew up. Note the chicken and dogs in this 1905 photograph. Below are workers' houses on Kitchens Lane, which got its name from the Kitchen family, who bought the Monastery mill and property in 1853. The two pairs of early-19th-century houses on Kitchens Lane fell into disrepair; one pair was removed in 1916. The family left the property when the Fairmount Park Commission appropriated their land in 1898.

Cresheim Farm at 425 Roumfort Road is one of the few remaining farmsteads that recall Mount Airy's rural past. Two original buildings, built on the property in 1700, were replaced by this substantial c. 1774 farmhouse, shown here around 1920 facing Cresheim Creek. Near the 1776 barn is a small quarry along Anderson Street. There the stone was dug to construct the buildings. Bought in 1830 by Col. Augustus Roumfort, the property extended to Mermaid Lane. (Antje Mattheus, David Kairys.)

The gate to the yard of the James Gorgas house is open in this photograph taken about 1888 at the northwest corner of Cresheim Road and Carpenter Lane, shortly before the house was demolished. The wall on the right was along the north side of the Phil-Ellena estate. (The Library Company of Philadelphia.)

In 1792, the Sebastian Unruh farmhouse, pictured here around 1911, was built at what is now 1011 Washington Lane. James Duval bought it in 1819. Charlotte Cushman, a well-known actress, later owned the house. Clementine Cope purchased it in 1885. The Cope family also owned 40 acres across Washington Lane and combined the properties to form Awbury Arboretum. Neighbors used part of this land for victory gardens during World War II, and it remains a community garden today. (Awbury Arboretum.)

Pictured here in 1890, this fine stone house once stood east of Chew Street, near Sharpnack Street. Peter Baker, a weaver, bought about 19 acres from blacksmith John Ashmead and his wife and built the house in 1721. In 1749, he sold it to merchant Joseph Marks, who added the front around 1750. Samuel Griffith bought the farmhouse as a summer residence in 1851. Much of Mount Airy remained rural during the 19th century.

Benjamin Chew, attorney general of the province of Pennsylvania, rented the Allen house in the summer of 1763, the year Edward Pennington advertised, "To be sold, a piece of land at the upper end of Germantown, with two small tenements thereon, containing eleven acres; it is pleasantly situated for a country seat; and there is a good orchard . . . a great variety of fruit trees of all kinds." Chew bought the land and built Cliveden in 1767. Walter Rogers Johnson took this daguerreotype of Cliveden in 1839, the same year the first photograph was made in the United States. Johnson had been the headmaster at Germantown Academy, where Chew was a trustee. Taken around 1875, the photograph at left shows probably Samuel Chew with a dog and two boys at a hammock. (Above, National Museum of American History; left, Library Company of Philadelphia.)

The Chew family lived at Cliveden for seven generations. In 1867, John Moran photographed James Smith, a servant of the Chew family for many years, on the front steps of Cliveden. Smith is believed to have been a slave who bought his freedom before coming to work for the Chews in 1819. He died around 1871. Below. the 18th-century Chew coach was photographed in the 1870s in front of Cliveden's barn. Edward Lamson Henry is pictured here. Samuel Chew commissioned him to paint the Battle of Germantown scene that is on display at Cliveden. The battle was fought in and around the Chew house in 1777. Unfortunately, this carriage burned in a 1970 barn fire. (Cliveden of the National Trust.)

In the 1700s, the Chew property extended to what is now Chew Avenue. In 1904, Mary Johnson Brown Chew donated Cliveden Park, at Chew and Johnson Streets, shown here in 1927, to the city. She stipulated that it "be maintained forever as a public park of as rustic a character as possible, and that no building, monument, statue . . . shall ever hereafter be erected." Today the District Community Action Council uses the house for the benefit of the community. (Philadelphia City Archives.)

East of Chew Street, where Sedgwick Street was later opened, was the Samuel Reaney farm, which had horses, cows, and orchards. The Sedgwick Farms development was later built on the site of this farm, seen here around 1900. Sedgwick Farms extended to Mount Pleasant Avenue, formerly a narrow dirt road leading to the Mount Pleasant station.

Two

GERMANTOWN AVENUE

This 1900 photograph shows the 1768 Johnson House at Germantown Avenue and Washington Lane. Quakers active in the abolition movement, the Johnson family used their house as a safe haven for people escaping slavery. Into the 1940s, corn was grown in the back lot, which extended to Cherokee Street. The Woman's Club of Germantown bought the house from the Johnson family in 1917, saving it from demolition. It was later sold to the Mennonite Church and now is an independent museum. (Historical Society of Pennsylvania.)

Built around 1760, the Ship House at 6338 Germantown Avenue was named for the plaster relief on the side of the building, reputedly added by a sea captain owner. The rear was constructed later as the area's first public hall, holding 250 people. The building became an inn, which was a stop for stagecoaches coming from Chestnut Hill to Philadelphia. In 1836, James Ford opened a ladies boarding school. Joshua Metzger, an American soldier, lived at 6336 Germantown Avenue (below). Reportedly, his wife, Elizabeth, and daughter melted down pewter spoons and teapots to form bullets for the American army. Jacob Unrod built the front section of the Metzger/Unrod house in 1806, using the older section in the back as a saddlery shop. Both houses were demolished in 1907 to make way for Pomona Street.

In the foreground are the Ship House (left) and the lawn of the estate Pomona Grove (right). Nine-year-old Jacob Keyser peeked out under the cellar door of the house on the right to see the Battle of Germantown raging in a field across the street. Between 1911 and 1923, the house was demolished to make way for East Duval Street. In 1916, a steam shovel unearthed the probable remains of soldiers buried there. (Historical Society of Pennsylvania.)

Around 1800, this house at 6358 Germantown Avenue was most likely built by William Keyser. The two bays were added around 1870. John Henry Sproegel lived in Germantown and was an early-18th-century owner of this lot. A German, he became a naturalized citizen of Great Britain in 1705.

John Johnson III built Upsala, a Federal-style house, at 6430 Germantown Avenue in 1798. His wife probably named it for the Swedish city of Uppsala. From this property, American troops fired cannons at the British seeking cover inside Cliveden across the street in 1777. Pictured here in 1891 are the garden and barn, now gone. Many generations of Johnsons lived here. Citizens rallied to save the house from demolition in 1943, and it is now administered by Cliveden.

The rear of this house at 6505 and 6507 Germantown Avenue is said to date from about 1727. It was called the Michael Billmeyer House after the printer who purchased it in 1789. In October 1777, Gen. George Washington was said to have used a spyglass to direct the Battle of Germantown from the house's front steps. An open field separated the house from Cliveden, where British troops were barricaded. To the left is a former pharmacy (see page 63).

The John Bardsley House at Germantown Avenue and Upsal Street was built as a frame house around 1760. A third story was added, visible on the building's south side. The city council hired Bardsley, a sign and house painter, around 1869 to bring back sparrows from his native England to destroy the rampant caterpillars then plaguing Philadelphia. This strategy backfired when sparrows edged out native songbirds. Below is another view of the Bardsley house, also taken about 1900, when it was the shop of watchmaker Charles Dar. Under a pocket watch–shaped sign, "Watchmaker and Jeweler Spectacles Repaired While You Wait" is painted on the windows. To the right is the Daniel Billmeyer house at 6504 Germantown Avenue. The rear was built around 1730, and the front was built in 1793. (Above, Historical Society of Pennsylvania.)

The front gate of the Germantown Church of the Brethren is all that remains today from this early-20th-century scene in the 6600 east block of Germantown Avenue. The house with the mansard roof in the foreground was demolished to make way for the opening of Montana Street. Wagon traffic was brisk on the avenue, but not as swift as the boy running on the right.

Across the street from the Church of the Brethren were these buildings north of Good Street. The tallest one is the Progress Steam Flour Mill. In the 1880s, when this image was made, mills no longer had to rely on surging creeks for power. A steam-powered mill could be located on more easily accessible "Main Street," as Germantown Avenue was called. In the distance is the stepped roofline of the building at 6620 Germantown Avenue, still there today.

George Bacon Wood took this photograph of his wife, Julia Reeve Wood, and others relaxing on the south side of his house at 6708 Germantown Avenue (see cover photograph). The two older women attend to their needlework, with a basket below, while the older man plays a small guitar. The house became part of the Phil-Ellena estate to the north and no longer stands. (The Library Company of Philadelphia.)

The Hesser/Bayard house once stood at 6749 Germantown Avenue across from the Pelham development. The 35-room house with extensive gardens and a greenhouse occupied several acres, as pictured below in a 1902 *Ladies Home Journal*. Reportedly, about 40 British soldiers buried were found when John Hesser excavated foundations for a new home after the Battle of Germantown in 1777, causing Hesser to build this house farther down the road. The house was demolished in 1907 to make way for a development of about 100 houses.

The architect Thomas Ustick Walter transformed an existing house at 7048 Germantown Avenue into a Greek Revival–style country home in 1835, with a colonnaded portico. It afforded a stunning view for its owners, George and Margaret Garrett, from the height of Mount Pleasant Avenue. Walter called it "Mr. Garrrett's Cottage," although it was named Hedge Bank. Walter designed the United States Capitol dome. In the 1850s, an unknown architect built an addition to the south, removed the portico, and updated the building's style to the then-fashionable Italianate style, seen in this 1871 photograph above. The barn probably dates from the 1700s. The Garretts' son, Thomas Hall Garrett, an analytical chemist, built 7010 Germantown Avenue next door (below). It was demolished in 1955 for the Acme Market. (Chestnut Hill Historical Society.)

The Farmers and Drovers Hotel at the northwest corner of Germantown Avenue and Carpenter Lane was unusually tall for a rural area. Farmers with produce-laden Conestoga wagons and drovers with cattle, sheep, and pigs to sell would stay overnight here. The sheds where animals were sheltered are to the right. This hotel was once the polling place for the northwest wards, including Chestnut Hill. It was demolished in 1894. The Engine No. 9 fire station now occupies the site.

The Mount Pleasant Inn, run by the Gorgas family, was a summer resort at the northwest corner of Germantown Avenue and Mount Pleasant Street on what was known as Garrett's Hill. On the first floor, Samuel Gorgas had a drugstore, which was replaced with Engard's Bakery, confectionery, and ice-cream parlor. It was demolished about 1923. (Chestnut Hill Historical Society.)

Around 1900, a trolley waits for a slower carriage to make its way south on Germantown Avenue, near the intersection with Mount Airy Avenue. The bell tower of the hall of the secret fraternal society, the Independent Order of Odd Fellows, is on the right, behind the trees. The first house on the right is 7127 Germantown Avenue. Both are still there today. East Durham Street was opened between 1911 and 1923 to the right of 7127 Germantown Avenue, where the fence is visible here. The porches of the Mount Pleasant Inn are on the left, with brick sidewalks and horse dung in the street. (Historical Society of Pennsylvania.)

This building was demolished in the first decade of the 20th century, and the Sedgwick Theatre replaced it in 1928. One can see the outline of the original one-and-a-half story house, built in 1750, on the facade on the right. A second story was added later. It was owned by George Carpenter in 1854 and the Brickhart family. Developers Ashton S. and Sedgwick C. Tourison hired William Lee to design the Sedgwick Theatre (left), at 7137 Germantown Avenue, in art deco style, photographed here in 1929. Roger's Produce Market's display is next door, and a boy is intent on the curbside construction. The film stopped rolling in the Sedgwick Theatre in 1967. (Above, Historical Society of Pennsylvania.)

In 1936, Sedgwick Chevrolet, located across the street from the Sedgwick Theatre, parked these two Chevrolets in the theater lobby as a promotional gimmick, which included a free variety show. Thomas Berkeley Garrett's dealership showroom (below) was outfitted with gas pumps on the sidewalk. The showroom enjoys new life as a fitness center today. (Sedgwick Cultural Center.)

Capt. Erasmus Pierce built what resembled a boat deck atop the roof of his "steamboat house." In the 1830s, Pierce tried unsuccessfully to establish a silk-growing business for his Philadelphia umbrella factory by planting mulberry trees here for silkworms. Thus, East Mount Pleasant Avenue appears as Mulberry Street on an 1860 map. During the Civil War, the Lutheran Orphans' Home used the house, hence the children pictured here. It was demolished in 1949. The Mount Airy Playground occupies the site today.

In this 1919 photograph, a stone, located on Germantown Avenue just below Mount Airy Avenue (see page 4), is inscribed with "7 to P" (seven miles to Philadelphia). Milestones, dating from 1801, measured the Germantown and Perkiomen Turnpike, which began at Vine and Third Streets, stretching to where Collegeville is today.

Charles Gorgas ran this store at 7238 Germantown Avenue, photographed around 1880. It was built about 1790. Gorgas was the postmaster, and when he died, his daughter took over. The Rittenhouse and Gorgas families owned the site until the 1940s, when the house was demolished for a Gulf station, now a Wawa market. The sale sign for this 1809 barn (below) along Allens Lane foreshadows its demolition to make way for an A&P Market parking lot in the 1950s. In 1948, the Glantz brothers bought the property in the foreground with the Sunoco sign and set up their MacLens auto body shop in the former stable of the Cresheim Arms Hotel (see page 108). The Italianate villa–style house across Germantown Avenue, Magnolia Villa, built in 1848 for James Gowen, remains as the Lutheran Theological Seminary's Hagan Hall. (Lutheran Archives Center at Philadelphia.)

The White Swan Hotel, with swan-shaped weather vane, was a tavern and stagecoach stop. The stage ended when railroads came around 1850. Cigars were made from locally grown tobacco on the site of what is now West Mount Airy Avenue. Farmers traveling to city markets sold sausage, eggs, butter, and chickens from the wagon sheds. Large herds filled Germantown Avenue on their way to overnight shelter behind the hotel. In 1929, the art deco Tourison Building replaced the hotel.

David Walters bought this Queen Anne–style house, built in 1886 at 7425 Germantown Avenue. Walters established a coal yard nearby, along the railroad tracks at Roumfort Road and Devon Street in the 1870s. (Richard Wood Snowden.)

Three

TRAINS AND TROLLEYS

Two horses pull a passenger car along rails on Germantown Avenue to the Philadelphia Centennial Exhibition in Fairmount Park in 1876. The Germantown Passenger Railroad Company line, built in 1859, terminated at the Pelham carbarn just above Phila-Ellena Street, the oldest building still owned by Southeastern Pennsylvania Transportation Authority (SEPTA) today. The trip between Eighth Street and Mount Airy took an amazingly fast 50 minutes. In the first year, 2,500 passengers rode daily. In 1894, the first trolleys replaced horsecars in Mount Airy.

When the Chestnut Hill Railroad line was constructed through the east side of Mount Airy in 1853, Mount Airy became more accessible to the downtown business district. In 1906, a crew prepares to eliminate the grade crossing. A railroad employee looks on from the crossing guard's shanty, left. The Gorgas Lane station, viewed looking east, was one of 125 stations designed by Frank Furness. Built in 1885, this station was demolished when the overpass for the railroad was built. (Philadelphia City Archives.)

Atop a freight car, a photographer took this image of the grade crossing at East Mount Airy Avenue in 1929. The crossing was converted to a bridge the following year. Seen beyond the plume of steam from the engine is the Sedgwick station's tower. Here two sidings left the main tracks: one for the Burnbest Coal Company and one for a lumberyard. The Philadelphia and Reading Railroad Company leased the Chestnut Hill Railroad line in 1870. (Ted Xaras.)

Around 1882, Frank Furness designed the Mount Pleasant station, seen here around 1905. In 1909, it was renamed Sedgwick Station after Sedgwick Farms, Ashton Tourison's development. Tourison convinced the president of the Philadelphia and Reading Railroad to eliminate the grade crossing, considered a menace by citizens, by lowering the road under the tracks at Sedgwick Street. The 1909 photograph below looks west under the tracks to the still sparsely developed east Mount Airy. The newly built Tudor-style houses at 224 and 222 East Sedgwick Street sit alone in a field. The Reading line was electrified in 1930. The station burned in 1981. (Above, Ted Xaras.)

Around 1898, two gentlemen hustle up the platform to meet the arriving steam engine at the Mount Airy station, which opened in 1883. It was designed by Frank Furness. The pavilion in the foreground and the long expanse of the station's roof sweeping down to form a porch were removed around 1930 when the level of the tracks was raised. The original station on this site was built in 1860 on land donated by James Gowen. As the competing Pennsylvania Railroad added a west line in 1884 through Mount Airy, the Reading Railroad upgraded its stations. Behind the station is a field where Devon Street houses will later stand. (J. M. Duffin.)

The Pennsylvania Railroad's Carpenter and Upsal stations served the handsome homes of the Pelham community and spurred the construction of more homes. Commercial buildings on Germantown Avenue filled in where there had been pastures and fields. This view of Carpenter station was taken about 1887, before the second floor was added to accommodate the station agent and his family in 1889. A man stands injudiciously on the trestle over Carpenter Lane as an inbound train approaches! (The Library Company of Philadelphia.)

On the site of the Mount Pleasant Arms apartments, at 265 West Mount Pleasant Avenue, Joseph W. Kennedy operated a coal, lime, and wood business in the 1890s. At several cross streets in Mount Airy, railroad sidings from both train lines were used for off loading coal to be delivered by wagon for home heating. The Pennsylvania Railroad line was electrified in 1931. (Chestnut Hill Historical Society.)

Allen Lane station was built as a one-story station, seen above between 1885 and 1889. The Rural Lane houses developed by Henry H. Houston are seen on the left beyond the house at 153 West Allens Lane. The chimney of the Mount Airy Waterworks rises to the right, where the Henry H. Houston School is today. Below, a steam engine pulls out of the Allen Lane station bound for Chestnut Hill, pulling the tender car for water and coal, one baggage car, and two passenger cars. The newspapers arrived by train twice a day. This photograph was taken after 1891, when Ashton Tourison built the second floor, and before 1912, when the arched pedestrian bridge over the tracks was added. Crops grow in a field on the west side of the tracks, where George Woodward built houses on Charlton Street in 1912. (Andrew Domanski.)

Just below Cresheim Creek ran the Fort Washington branch of the Pennsylvania Railroad. It turned off from the west line above Allens Lane and operated from 1893 until 1952. The early-19th-century house at 7627 Germantown Avenue was the Germantown Avenue railroad station, pictured here in 1935. It exists today without the porch. Steps lead up to the train platform, alongside a billboard that reads, "Oh the object of my affection is gasoline perfection Gulf." In 1910, before any other lines were electrified in the Philadelphia area, a newspaper article announced the Cresheim branch would operate with electric batteries, replacing steam. The Pennsylvania Highway Route 309 was built on part of the former six-mile track bed. Below, the rail line runs under Stenton Avenue and over the creek, with open pastures beyond to the east. (Above, Philadelphia City Archives.)

This trolley, pictured above around 1895 beside the Pelham carbarn on Germantown Avenue, was built in 1894 to go as far as Rex Avenue in Chestnut Hill. The front of the trolley had a rope fender to scoop people out of danger. In 1944, Philadelphia transit systems stopped operating because of a strike due to an order to instruct African Americans in train operation. The United States Army sent 5,000 troops to Philadelphia. Some of the troops camped by the Lovett Memorial Library and guarded the Pelham carbarn. Soldiers were stationed on the cars running on Germantown Avenue for about two weeks until the crisis was averted. Below, around 1899, is an open-air trolley at the corner of Germantown and Gowen Avenues, with the Lutheran Theological Seminary grounds behind, before this corner was cut back to widen the intersection in the 1920s. (Above, Chestnut Hill Historical Society; below, J. M. Duffin.)

Four

ESTATES

Pomona Grove was built in 1755 by Samuel Shoemaker on the 6300 block of Germantown Avenue. In 1811, James Duval, a retired French merchant, bought the 20-acre property and expanded the house and orchards. For Amos Little, a Philadelphia Centennial Exhibition commissioner, it became a summer home in 1875. In 1886, Little sold more than 11 acres to be developed into building lots, and Pomona and Duval Streets were opened. Pictured here in 1889, it was gone the next year.

West Mount Airy in the mid-19th century was dominated by the 350-acre George Carpenter estate, called Phil-Ellena ("for the love of Ellen") after his second wife. Born in Germantown, a carpenter's son, he returned to the Germantown Township to build his estate. Three gates and an ornamental fence with 14 massive urns faced Germantown Avenue. The mansion's observatory may be seen in the photograph below from about 1887. Carpenter made a fortune with the inspired *Carpenter's Family Medicine Chest Dispensatory*, a book accompanied by medicines, targeted at rural families without ready access to doctors. He invested in real estate around Philadelphia, owning over 500 acres in the Germantown/Mount Airy area. (The Library Company of Philadelphia.)

The then-popular Greek Revival–style house, with matching porticos front and back, took three years to build (from 1841 to 1844). In the center of the roof was an octagonal observatory. From it, vessels on the Delaware River eight miles away could be seen. The opulent interiors included the drawing room (below), art gallery, library, and conservatory. George Carpenter died in 1860 at the age of 58. He lived at Phil-Elena for only 16 years. Ellen and their children lived there until 1893. At that time, a three-day auction was held to sell the contents. Developers considered using the house as an inn. In February 1897, it was one of the last buildings on the grounds to be razed.

The grounds of Phil-Ellena were strewn with assorted features, including a Greek temple–style doghouse, greenhouses, two lakes, a racecourse, and gardens. Seen above around 1887, a natural history museum displayed specimens of ornithology, mineralogy, geology, entomology, and zoology (note two stuffed dogs in the foreground), plus Native American relics and a room for beekeeping. George Carpenter was an early supporter of the Academy of Natural Sciences, to which his wife eventually presented his collections. A fanciful, Italianate-style clock tower (left) stood 65 feet tall. Residents of Mount Airy grew accustomed to its hourly "dong, dong." When the new Pelham development closed around it, one reporter wrote, "As though feeling out of place in the development of the building-lot era, the old clock now strikes the hour at eccentric intervals." The clock tower survived until 1902. (Above, The Library Company of Philadelphia.)

A man grooms a horse outside the large horse and cow stable on the Carpenter estate, probably in 1887. By 1896, Cresheim Road was opened across the grounds, and the barn was converted to a house for the Heppe family and called Barnhurst (below). Later it became the convent building for the Sisters of St. Joseph in connection with the Cecilian Academy. At 6818 Cresheim Road, it is the only Phil-Ellena building still standing.

Around 1860, English immigrant Thomas Drake, who made a fortune with textile mills that manufactured the popular Kentucky Jean, built this mansion, Montebello, on about seven acres at the northeast corner of East Washington Lane at Morton Street. He and his daughter, Charlotte Drake Cardeza, a survivor of the sinking of the *Titanic*, traveled the world on safari. The Drake/Cardeza family maintained its own menagerie, including bear, elk, and buffalo (pictured below in 1902) and kennels for breeding Great Dane dogs. The house was demolished in 1940 for row houses. (Above, Andrew Jarvis.)

Head gardener Edward Jones stands beside the Liberty Bell with 1776 below sculpted in flowers. It was one of many elaborate floral creations on the grounds of Montebello, seen looming behind. Around 1900, Jones lived in row houses nearby on Duval Street and later on Pomona Street, erected on the old Pomona Grove estate. (Cynthia Best.)

East of the Drake/Cardeza house, just west of Chew Street, was the Christian Ross house, site of the notorious 1874 kidnapping of four-year-old Charley Ross, who was never returned although the ransom was paid. Many people would later claim to be Charley, but the family never accepted these claims. From 1916 to 1925, the house was used for the Cliveden Presbyterian Church. Then a sanctuary replaced the house. In 1978, the church disbanded, selling the building.

In 1887, on five acres of the former Carpenter estate, Cornelius N. Weygandt, president of the Western National Bank, built Uwchllan, designed by George Pearson and pictured here in 1899, at 229 West Upsal Street. Fabulous gardens, with tropical plants in containers, surrounded the house, which later became the Pilling house. Weygandt's son, Dr. Cornelius Weygandt, a professor at the University of Pennsylvania, wrote a book on the Wissahickon area and other local histories. A 100-unit apartment building, Pelham Park apartments, took its place around 1946. (Below, Chestnut Hill Historical Society.)

At Wissahickon Avenue and Washington Lane is the Thomas Mansion. In the 1850s, machine tool manufacturer George Clifford Thomas acquired 23 acres, which became Clifford Park. He built this suburban mansion in 1869 in a still rural part of the city, before Lincoln Drive was opened below it. In 1912, the estate was bequeathed to Fairmount Park. Pictured here in 1918 is the Aucott family, who, from 1882, lived in the Blue Bell Hill neighborhood across the street at 6204 Wissahickon Avenue. Eugene Aucott, on the lower right, had just been christened. He lived his entire life there until 2002. (Edwin D. Aucott.)

Park Gate is the name of the Henry McIlhenny house at Johnson Street, above Lincoln Drive. The Fairmount Park gates exist today but without the wood trellis, seen here in 1911. Henry's father, John McIlhenny, was a successful manufacturer of gas meters and outfitted the house in European art treasures. His son collected works by Paul Cezanne, Edgar Degas, and Pablo Picasso, and American artists, such as Franklin Watkins and Marsden Hartley. Today the house, owned by the Philadelphia School District, is abandoned and overgrown.

Saracinesca, designed by Hazelhurst and Huckel, was built in 1892 at 701 West Allens Lane. Harlan Page, its owner, was president of the Abrasive Company, which manufactured grinding wheels in Bridesburg. His contribution to the fledgling Summit Presbyterian Church in 1895 enabled the church to be built. The porch and flaring stairs of the house are gone today. The conical top of the tower was replaced with a flat, crenellated top, and the castlelike top above the arched windows has been removed. The house included a billiard room, library, music room, and nine bedrooms. Below, family members pose beside the east facade of the house in a carriage with a matched pair of horses.

Since 1953, the Allens Lane Art Center has occupied the carriage house of this mansion. Its name, Medloch Wold, is carved into the stone gatepost along Allens Lane and means "medieval lake and wood." In the 1880s, Henry H. Houston bought property to develop in west Mount Airy. Houston sold this 10-acre tract to Henry Tetlow, a manufacturer of perfumes and toiletries, who built this mansion, with a pond, along McCallum Street, pictured here in 1896. In 1905, George Vare, a state senator, bought the property as a summer retreat. In the 1920s, Gertrude Houston Woodward, Henry's daughter, feared it would be developed into apartments. She worked to consolidate Saracinesca and Medloch Wold, demolishing the latter for a playground and tennis courts and keeping the carriage house, pictured below in 1945, for changing rooms and a theater. That year, Woodward donated it to Fairmount Park. (Below, Allens Lane Art Center.)

This photograph shows the rear view of 405 East Gowen Avenue, the home of the Kolb family, between 1911 and 1919. It was built in 1889 and remodeled in the Tudor style around 1905. Charles Kolb owned Kolb's Bakeries, which made Bond Bread in Center City Philadelphia. The grounds extended to Roumfort Road, Crittenden Street, and Stenton Avenue, with extensive gardens (below) and a large greenhouse filled with carnations. The gardens were replaced in the 1950s with scores of smaller houses. The carriage house, built in 1906, can be found at 7409 Crittenden Street. The girl and two women in both photographs are presumably Kolbs. (J. M. Duffin.)

Five

MOUNT AIRY AT WORK

The Livezey Mill along the east side of the Wissahickon, photographed in 1889, was in Roxborough Township. The ridge above, here a pasture, was in Mount Airy. Remnants of its walls can be found near the Wissahickon Creek. This mill business, said to be the largest in the colonies, was supplemented with wine and barrel making and grain sales. Although the main business was grinding wheat into flour, the mill also ground spices and flax (to make linseed oil for paint). In the early 19th century, the Wissahickon valley supported at least 20 mills because it combined waterpower with a location along one of the main arteries into Philadelphia. To the left behind the trees is the house, Glen Fern.

Thomas Shoemaker owned this site and probably built the center section of this house by 1746. The following year, he sold it and a mill to Thomas Livezey, whose Quaker family came from England in 1682. Livezey named the house Glen Fern. A poet, he wrote in 1767, "Near Wissahickon's mossy banks, where purling fountains glide, Beneath the spruces' shady boughs, and laurels' blooming pride . . . I drink the wine my hills produce, on wholesome food I dine, My little offspring round me are like clusters on the vine." Three additions were added to the structure during the 123 years the family prospered here. Beginning in 1869, the City of Philadelphia bought the site for inclusion in Fairmount Park, and the mill buildings were removed "to enhance a picturesque ideal then favored." Below, this barn stood up a rise from the house. (Above, Chestnut Hill Historical Society; below, Free Library of Philadelphia.)

Farmers' wagons could be seen backed up along the mile between the mill and Germantown Avenue. Livezey kept a team of horses to supplement the farmers' teams hauling heavy, barreled flour up the steep bank of the Wissahickon Creek gorge. Pictured here around 1900, this wagon has just finished the long climb from the mill up to Livezey Lane, now Allens Lane. The second Livezey barn, built in the late 18th century and surviving today, is seen in the background. In the photograph below, taken in the 1890s, Sarah Livezey Firth stands in front of the second family house, built about 1760 and called Fairview, at 911 Allens Lane. The family moved there after Glen Fern was appropriated. Ten generations of Livezeys have lived on this land up to today. (Livezey family.)

Paper Mill Run, also known as the Monoshone Creek, branched off from the Wissahickon Creek under what is now Lincoln Drive. It provided power for the Glen Echo Carpet Mills, seen here around 1890. The mill was located north of Carpenter Street (now Lane), between what are now McCallum and Emlen Streets along what became the path of Lincoln Drive. Erected in 1812 or 1813, it was used by various businesses. In 1830, William McCallum rented it for the manufacture of carpets, and a year later, with his brother Andrew, bought the building and 20 acres. The mill was converted to steam in 1835; 100 men were employed. In 1883, the mill business, then known as McCallum, Crease, and Sloan, moved to Wayne Junction in lower Germantown. The buildings were demolished between 1895 and 1906. (Historical Society of Pennsylvania.)

In 1824, Jacob Derr purchased this property at the southeast corner of Germantown and Mount Pleasant Avenues and ran a carriage-making, wheelwright, and blacksmith's shop in the rear. His sons George and Charles continued running the shop through most of the 19th century. A specialized blacksmith was needed to fashion the ironwork for carriage underbodies, braces, and hinges. Twin houses fronting on Mount Pleasant Avenue replaced these buildings between 1906 and 1911. The Mount Airy Presbyterian Church chapel (page 77) can be seen beyond in this photograph taken between 1894 and 1901. Below is George Waldman's carriage factory at 86 and 88 West Johnson Street in 1899. Not wanting to lose any business to the new invention, he advertised in 1907 that he could design and build automobile bodies and repaint and repair their woodwork. (Above, Historical Society of Pennsylvania.)

English-born Thomas Meehan came to America in 1848 and for a time worked at Bartram's Garden in southwest Philadelphia. Franklinville, later part of Mount Airy, became Meehan's home. A botanist, nurseryman, and councilman, he worked to improve public schools and establish small parks. Meehan's nursery in Mount Airy started in 1854. In 1868, he bought the Jacob Hortter farm, east of Chew Street (later Avenue), expanding it to 75 acres, seen here in 1899. William Saunders, noted Scottish landscape designer, was his partner briefly. A prolific writer, Meehan published *Meehan's Monthly*, and *The American Handbook of Ornamental Trees*, influencing taste and design. Meehan corresponded with Charles Darwin and was interested in the theory of evolution. Below, men work in what had become the largest nursery in America. Plants were shipped to Europe, Australia, South Africa, and South America. On Sundays, neighbors strolled among the acres of trees, shrubs, and plants.

The office of Mount Airy Nurseries was in the 7300 block of Germantown Avenue with this Pennsylvania School for the Deaf building behind. It was adjacent to the Cresheim Cottage, on the site of present-day West Gowen Avenue. Townsend Ward wrote in 1869 about the nursery of Charles H. Miller, "to whose taste Chestnut Hill is not a little indebted." Miller, the chief of the Bureau of Horticulture for the Philadelphia Centennial Exhibition in 1876, designed a site plan for John Morris in Chestnut Hill. This site later became the Morris Arboretum.

In 1761, cabinetmaker Jacob Knorr began a carpentry business that would become Kirk and Nice. The business occupied the old building seen here on the left, at 6301 Germantown Avenue. Around 1870, the firm stopped making furniture to concentrate on making coffins and to transition into undertaking. The firm demolished this building in 1875 to build a new one, which it occupied until 2000, when this branch closed. This 1859 photograph shows the Washington Tavern on the right.

Two fire horns and a date stone of 1878 adorn the top floor of 6825 Germantown Avenue, one of the first fire stations built after the Philadelphia Fire Department was formed in 1871. In 1902, this station became a store after Engine No. 9 station moved across the street to bigger quarters below. The Germantown Township was divided into three fire company jurisdictions in 1764. The Upper Ward Company became the Franklin Fire Company on Germantown Avenue near Franklin Street, now Hortter. In 1804, the Mount Airy Engine Company was organized on Germantown Avenue, at Miller's Lane, now Gowen Avenue. It disbanded in 1871 with the advent of the professional fire department. In the early years, each resident was required to have two leather fire buckets ready in their house to form a line from a pond or well in case of fire. (Above, McCoubrey/Overholser.)

In 1872, this former Mount Airy School building along Allens Lane was converted to an engine house for the Philadelphia Water Department. Seen here around 1905, it powered pumps for the adjacent Mount Airy Waterworks reservoir, built in 1853. The Henry H. Houston School was built on the site of the reservoir and this building in 1927. (Historical Society of Pennsylvania.)

Warren Poley built this pharmacy at 6519 Germantown Avenue in 1880 and had a second store at Walnut Lane. "Poley's Lavodent . . . toothpaste. Guaranteed to be perfectly harmless, and to thoroughly cleanse and disinfect the teeth, perfume the breath," was advertised. Cream sodas in the first decade of the 20th century cost a nickel at the soda fountain. Pharmacist Norman Reibstein owned the store by 1956, and a school bought it from his widow in 1995. (Project Learn School.)

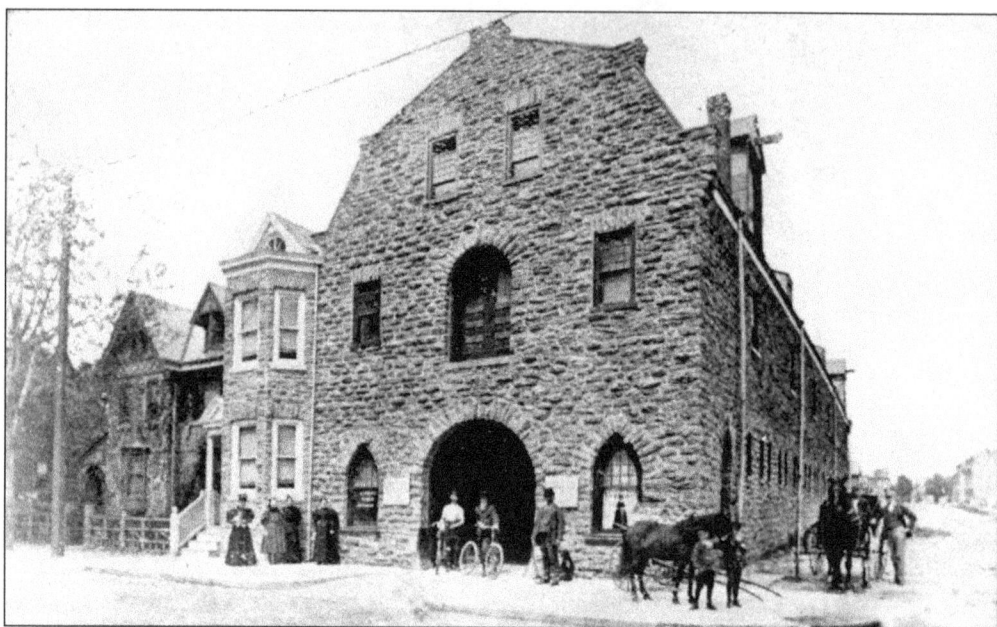

In the 1890s, when this photograph was taken, W. M. McKeon was the proprietor of the Palace Livery Stable at the northeast corner of Greene and Duval Streets. In the increasingly densely-built neighborhood, residents found it convenient to board their horses. Horses were sold here too. It was converted into a garage in the second decade of the 20th century. A gas pump was installed at the corner after it became a gas station. The building survived past 1979.

A 1913 booklet written by J. Gordon Baugh Jr., commemorating the 50th anniversary of the Emancipation Proclamation, included this image of the black-owned Wissahickon Garage at 730 Carpenter Street as a new enterprise. Its owner, James Robinson, had been working on cars since 1911. In the early 20th century, as automobile use increased, commercial garages not only repaired cars but also stored and leased them. The building survives today.

Leander Pierce (in chauffeur's uniform) poses with a 1913 Cadillac at its garage on Johnson Street at the corner of Cherokee Street, the former site of George Waldman's carriage factory (see page 59). Born in Salem, New Jersey, he, his wife, Laura, and their family lived at 49 West Duval Street near the garage. His employer, Mrs. Malcolm, lived at the Emlen Arms Apartments, 6733 Emlen Street, seven blocks from the garage. (Pierce/Cuff/Harris/Mack family.)

The third location of Groben's Seafood market was on Phil-Ellena Street across from St. Michael's Lutheran Church cemetery. This four-generation business, dating from 1877, originated in Germantown. After suspending operation during World War II, the Grobens moved it to 6833 Germantown Avenue in 1959. Chauffeurs would drive up and ring a bell on a post outside to pick up their orders. The business was sold in 2006 and continues to sell to local restaurants and the public. (Atwater Kent Museum.)

E. K. Paul Hardware was at 6837 to 6839 Germantown Avenue for 139 years, beginning in 1859. After buying the business in 1915, Charles Gable gave it a new look with two one-story storefronts with skylights. Sons Charles Jr. and Albert joined the business in the 1940s. Below is the interior of 6839 Germantown Avenue sometime after the reconstruction. Ladders on a track ran the length of the store for difficult-to-reach items on the upper shelves. Sterling Dorsheimer and Charles Clark took over in 1980 and closed the doors in 1998. (Chestnut Hill Historical Society.)

Fred MacFarland's barbershop opened at 7112 Germantown Avenue in 1903. He soon moved across the street to 7149 Germantown Avenue, living with his family above the shop. Regular customers had their own shaving mugs lined up on the shelves. His card advertised that he made house calls: "Families Waited Upon at Home." Patrons were warned to heed the sign, "Please do not use Profanity," when the students from the Lutheran Theological Seminary came in. Below, fourth from the right, Don Murphy was hired in 1954 and took over the shop in 1986. In the foreground is a carousel horse, made down the road at the Philadelphia Toboggan Company. Children rode on it when getting haircuts. The cash register and the little barrel containing lollipops for children have been there since before 1954. (Right, Chestnut Hill Historical Society; below, Don Murphy.)

Henry Auchy and Chester Albright opened the Philadelphia Toboggan Company workshop at 130 East Duval Street in a converted stable. They made carousels and roller coasters, called toboggans, for amusement parks nationwide. Where real horses once lived, fanciful steeds were hand carved and painted. Local children delighted to watch them being loaded onto freight trains at Germantown station. The *Germantown Guide* reported the firm's artists "would well decorate the parlors of our homes." (Tom Rebbie, Philadelphia Toboggan Coasters Corporation.)

Rothe Florists, founded by Max Rothe, celebrates its centennial year in 2008. It has continued for four generations. The original one-story florist shop is seen here around 1950 at 7150 Germantown Avenue. The family lived in the house next door. Herbert Rothe Sr. moved the business into the house in 1956. Sebastian Unruh bought the land in 1781 and afterward built this house. (Rothe family.)

Easter flowers, ready to be delivered, fill one of the 13 greenhouses behind the store. Members of the Max Rothe family and their workers pose here, probably between 1911 and 1919. Some workers were recent immigrants from Germany. Below is a view of the greenhouses in the 1940s or 1950s. The Odd Fellows hall tower at Germantown and Mount Airy Avenues and the Schaeffer-Ashmead Memorial Lutheran Church tower at the Lutheran Theological Seminary may be seen on the horizon. The 13 greenhouses were demolished in 1985, and the land was sold to the city for a municipal parking lot. (Rothe family.)

Abram Engard's Bakery moved from the first floor of the Mount Pleasant Hotel two blocks south to this building at the southwest corner of Germantown and Mount Airy Avenues in 1895. Developer Ashton S. Tourison was responsible for the spate of new commercial buildings in the Mount Airy business center. The first was this building at 7174 Germantown Avenue, with a conical turret, that housed the bakery. Still there today in the basement are the ovens pictured here with the bakers. (P. J. McMenamin.)

This cart advertised for the bakery in the early 20th century. Seen below in 1950, Bridget and Patrick McMenamin bought a bar business in 1936 at 7222 Germantown Avenue. It relocated to 7170 Germantown Avenue in 1939. Bridget was a licensed bartender, unusual for a woman at the time. She worked from 7:00 a.m. to noon, a time when factory workers from Germantown were thirsty. Women entered only at the "Ladies Entrance" sign by the side door. A jukebox is visible in the back center. The family lived upstairs, often with extended family newly arrived from Ireland in the 1940s and 1950s. In 1942, Patrick McMenamin bought the bakery building at 7174 Germantown Avenue. The third generation of McMenamins runs the bar and restaurant today. (P. J. McMenamin.)

Here architect Frank Miles Day designed a home and studios amid the ruins of a burned farmhouse. He retained the barn, renovating it into three studios for painters Violet Oakley, Jessie Willcox Smith, and Elizabeth Shippen Green. When the three artists and their housemate, Henrietta Cozens, lost their home in Villanova in 1906, family friend Dr. George Woodward offered this site along the Cresheim Creek, photographed by Green in 1907. So grateful were the new tenants that in 1925, they renamed West Gowen Avenue St. George's Road. They named their new home Cogslea, an acronym from the first letters of their last names plus "lea," referring to the surrounding meadows. Violet Oakley had the largest studio, depicted at left in 1910. She had many mural commissions, including the Pennsylvania State Capitol and Vassar College Alumnae House. (Richard Wood Snowden.)

Artis T. Ray Sr. moved with his family from South Carolina to Philadelphia, attended Temple University, studying music and chemistry, and then worked at the Frankford Arsenal. In 1945, Ray began a cosmetics manufacturing business, Ramo Beauty and Barber Supply Company, aimed at the black consumer. It occupied garages behind his and his wife Louetta's house at 319 East Upsal Street, built by his father-in-law, William Byrd. Eugene Webb, a beautician, demonstrates Ramo products at a trade convention in Philadelphia around 1959. All four children helped with the business while they kept up their grades in preparation for college. Daughters Louise, Louetta, and Olga sometimes posed as models. Artis Ray Jr. (right) leans against one of the trucks used to deliver the supplies. The products were sold nationally, making Ray a successful entrepreneur. (Louetta Ray Hadley.)

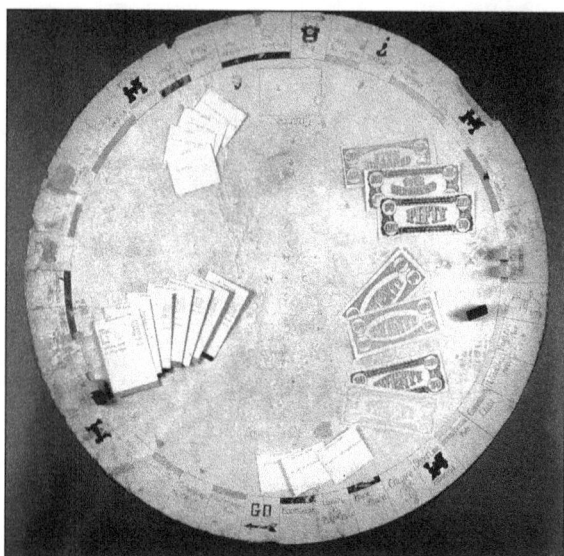

Charles Darrow of 40 Westview Street made this unique round Monopoly board in 1933. It was copied from the Landlord's Game, which Lizzie Magie had patented in 1904 as a teaching tool for Henry George's radical, free-market economics. Darrow appropriated the game from Charles Todd, manager at nearby Emlen Arms apartments, who got it from a Westtown School friend. Darrow marketed it successfully and then collaborated with Parker Brothers to make a fortune from the best-selling game in the world. (Forbes Collection.)

In 1954, one could buy beer in the Lincoln Drive Delicatessen at Mount Pleasant Avenue. Owners Samuel and Elizabeth Feldman posed with customer Jane Johnson, center, below an early television set. Sitting here, Elizabeth would peel the potatoes for her popular potato salad. They operated the business from 1940 to 1964. They soon regretted selling it and bought it back, operating it until 1975 and advertising outside with a sign, "Under Old Management." (Debbie Feldman.)

Six

INSTITUTIONS

Twenty families of the Church of the Brethren, also called Dunkers, arrived in the upper part of the Germantown Township in 1719. They had been persecuted by the authorities in the area of Krefeld, Lower Rhine. Adult baptism by immersion was practiced in the Wissahickon near Kitchens Lane. The Brethren were pacifists, wore plain garb, and refused to swear oaths. In 1760, the congregation built a log meetinghouse, the first site of this denomination in America, replaced in 1770 by this stone building, now 6611 Germantown Avenue. The church officially forbade slavery among its members in 1782, long before the nation did.

Mount Airy Presbyterian Church began in 1880 in the building at 115 and 117 East Mount Airy Avenue, transformed long ago into the house below. The United Brethren in Christ had built the church, but reportedly the congregation broke up in 1879 over "the question of amusements and frivolous living." In 1884, the Presbyterians moved to the northeast corner of Germantown and Mount Pleasant Avenues. (Below, Mount Airy Presbyterian Church.)

George Pearson designed this chapel, pictured here in 1895, at the back of the property, anticipating a time when a bigger sanctuary would be built for the Mount Airy Presbyterian Church. The sexton's house is on the left. The chapel's interior is shown below. In 1901, Joseph Huston designed the present church. The chapel was demolished in 1956 to make way for a Sunday school building. (Mount Airy Presbyterian Church.)

St. Michael's Lutheran Church at 6671 Germantown Avenue was the first German Lutheran church in Philadelphia. The first building was erected in 1730 and replaced by this structure in 1819. It was leveled for a Gothic Revival sanctuary in 1897. A Sunday school building was constructed to the right in 1886, after this photograph was taken. As early as the 1740s, a school was reported to be at St. Michael's. Services were held in German until the late 1830s.

The Episcopal Grace Church first occupied this 1858 building on East Mount Airy Avenue. Holy Cross Catholic Church is on this site today. When Holy Cross was established in 1890, the congregation took over this building. It served as its worship space until 1910, when the Holy Cross School was built to the east. The congregation worshipped in the school until the present church was erected in 1929. (Grace Epiphany Church.)

The cornerstone of Grace Church was laid in 1888 in a ceremony amid braced window frames. Franklin B. Gowen, president of the Philadelphia and Reading Railroad, donated the site, a part of his family's land holdings that he was developing into an affluent suburb. One can see the open land beyond. Renowned ecclesiastical architect Charles M. Burns Jr. designed the church. The sanctuary is adorned with stained-glass windows by several well-known companies, including Tiffany Studios. Below is a view in 1889, before the parish house and rectory were built in 1890 and 1891. After a fire in the Church of the Epiphany at Lincoln Drive and Carpenter Lane, they consolidated in 1991. (Grace Epiphany Church.)

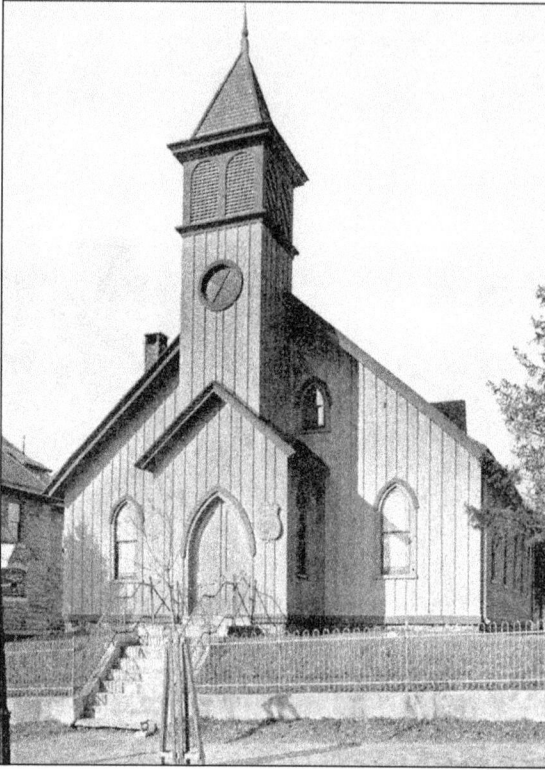

Before the Mount Pleasant Avenue Methodist Episcopal Church built this chapel in 1877, the congregation met for three years in the second floor of the Odd Fellows hall at Germantown and Mount Airy Avenues as a mission of the Haines Street Church. The present building was built in 1905. Now without a congregation, it operates as a day care center.

In 1885 Summit Presbyterian Church first met in a small building at Greene Street and Carpenter Lane, where Weaver's Way Co-Op is today, for prayer meetings and Sunday school, when western Mount Airy was becoming more densely developed. Trustees for the Pelham development gave the land for the church. On the left, the church, fronting on Westview Street near Greene Street, was completed in 1895. In 1911, Carl Ziegler designed a bigger church, pictured here before the tower was added in 1922.

The Second Baptist Church of Germantown at Upsal Street and Germantown Avenue began as a mission Sunday school in 1859. The congregation purchased land from the Chew estate, and in 1866, the chapel was built at the rear of the property. The sanctuary was added in 1881. The church burned in 1930 but was rebuilt. After another fire in 1970, only the three arched doorways of the nave and the rear portion survived, so the congregation meets in the chapel.

St. Madeleine Sophie Catholic Church began in this house at 6455 Germantown Avenue in 1926, converted into a school and convent. The parishioners worshiped at the Pelham Theater at Germantown Avenue and Sharpnack Street while a new church site was sought. Every Sunday, the sisters brought an organ in a wheelbarrow and set up an improvised altar. A new church was built on Greene Street in 1930. Sacred Heart Manor nursing home replaced this house around 1960. (St. Madeleine Sophie Church.)

Grace Baptist Church was organized in 1892, and its 34 East Sharpnack Street site was purchased in 1896. This one-story structure was built here in 1908. It was replaced by the structure there today, whose cornerstone reads 1915. In 1960, the growing church bought a bigger site for a new church on West Johnson Street. At left, Lilinau Valentine and Rudolph Goffney were wed at Grace Baptist in 1952. The reception was held at the Pyramid Club, a social club for black men in Center City. Lilinau taught Sunday school, later becoming a schoolteacher. She lived on Duval Street and graduated from Germantown High School in 1944. At Germantown High, she joined the Fellowship Club, in which groups of three students, one black, one white Christian, and one Jew, attempted to create understanding by speaking at other schools. (Left, Lilinau V. Goffney.)

In the 1930s, Jewish business and professional people met monthly as a cultural association. In 1936, this group became the Germantown Jewish Centre, first meeting in the Automobile Club of Germantown on Emlen Street. The school, on the right, was built in 1947 on the former Glen Echo Carpet Mills property, followed by the synagogue in 1951. Rabbi Elias Charry and other religious leaders led an effort to persuade white residents not to leave the city. Many citizens worked to create a stable, integrated community. (Germantown Jewish Centre.)

Built in 1740, one of the oldest surviving buildings in northwest Philadelphia is the Beggarstown School at 6669 Germantown Avenue. It originally was a school for St. Michael's Lutheran Church. Subjects were taught in German. In 1817, the first Sunday school in the area met here to address problems with neighborhood children stealing fruit from orchards and damaging property. The building is pictured here before 1910.

In 1775, the Concord School at 6313 Germantown Avenue was built, named after the Battle of Concord. It served students who lived too far from the Union School (later Germantown Academy). The school taught only in English, reflecting the trend away from German. The school closed in 1865, when public schools opened. The Concord School is on the site of the Upper Burying Ground, sometimes called Ax's Burying Ground. It was begun in 1693 and contains graves dating from 1716.

Florence Tourison Reid (in the plaid skirt) went to the school in Ruth Haughenbaugh's home at the southeast corner of Musgrave Street and Gorgas Lane in the 1890s. The smallest scholar in the front row was unable to keep still for the long exposure of the camera.

With only four classrooms, the public Franklin School, built in 1862 at Phil-Ellena and Musgrave Streets, reflected the sparse population in this part of the township. In 1892, the Andrew Curtin School (below) was built beside the Franklin School on the 6000 block of Musgrave. In the 1920s, the school's white teachers taught black and white students in kindergarten through third grade. Agatha Baul Valentine and her four sisters walked home for lunch to West Duval Street and back everyday. In 1927, the Eleanor Cope Emlen School was built on Chew Street. Curtin became a school for students with learning difficulties and was eventually abandoned. Only the iron fence posts seen in both photographs remain today. (Above, Philadelphia City Archives.)

Pictured here is the Mount Airy School, built on the south side of Allens Lane in 1872, with four classrooms per floor. The first school at Allens and Rural Lanes was built across the street in 1798 on land donated by Andrew Allen. It was destroyed by fire in 1851, and then a small building was erected on the site (see page 63). (Philadelphia City Archives.)

Edith Willard's eighth-grade class at the Henry H. Houston School posed proudly at graduation in 1951. Principal Mary Gibbs is in the center of the group, with teacher Edith Willard to the right. In the front row, twin sisters Ruth and Rita Dunning are dressed identically, even their necklaces. The Henry H. Houston School, named for the Pennsylvania Railroad executive and developer, opened in 1927. (Debbie Feldman.)

The Charles W. Henry School at Carpenter Lane and Greene Street opened in 1908 and was considered immense. Caroline Moffet was a teacher at the Carpenter School across the street. That school, in the old Summit Presbyterian Church building, preceded the Henry School. Moffet became the first principal at Henry, retiring in 1936. Its annex, the Alfred Crease School on Wissahickon Avenue, closed in 1956. Caroline Moffett influenced Fairmount Park to establish a bird sanctuary in Carpenter's Woods in 1921. In 1925, a bird museum opened at 7005 Wissahickon Avenue, in the park next door to her home at 7001 Wissahickon Avenue (both now gone). Moffet also founded the Wissahickon Bird Club, which later merged with the Friends of the Wissahickon. Below, in 1926, Henry School students made birdhouses, grew bird food, and more. (Above, Philadelphia City Archives.)

In 1879, Frank Furness designed this house, Cresheim, for Franklin B. Gowen, president of the Philadelphia and Reading Railroad, along Roumfort Road where Crest Park Road is today. William Steel later owned the house. It became Miss Mills School, "the first out-of-door school for well children," in 1917. Lessons were taught in open-air shelters on the 10-acre property (below) in the belief that young lungs would benefit from cold, pure winter air. The school's day and boarding students used the campus as an outdoor classroom as they learned beekeeping, sketching, horseback riding, and nature study using the Cresheim Creek. The school, founded in 1906, originally operated at 7417 Boyer Street and then at 302 Gowen Avenue.

Margaret Potter, Rev. Simeon Hill, and Louisa Lovett founded the Mount Airy Free Library in a rented room at a lumberyard in 1885. Louisa's aunt Charlotte Lovett Bostwick built the Memorial Free Library in 1887, changed to Lovett Memorial Free Library in 1894. Ashton Tourison designed it as a memorial to her brother Capt. Thomas R. Lovett. He had bequeathed her the land on the east side of Germantown Avenue above and below Sedgwick Street, seen here in 1927. During World War I, the board authorized the planting of a war garden in Lovett Park. In 1924, the board erected a monument to the 34 people from Mount Airy who died in the war. It was a massive stone from Valley Forge with a bronze tablet, which was stolen in the 1970s. Lovett became a branch of the Free Library of Philadelphia in 1924. Below is the original reading room. (Above, Philadelphia City Archives; below, Lovett Memorial Library.)

The Pennsylvania Institution for the Dumb and Deaf (the name changed to Pennsylvania School for the Deaf in 1934) was built at 7500 Germantown Avenue on 60 acres purchased from Henry H. Houston. The buildings were designed by Cope and Stewardson and the Wilson Brothers and used Wissahickon schist stone, quarried on the site. The school, founded in 1820 in Center City Philadelphia, is the third-oldest school for the deaf in the nation. In 1892, it moved to this larger campus on the former farm of William Schaeffer, a horticulturist specializing in chestnut trees, and president of the Pennsylvania Horticultural Society for 14 years. The farmhouse at 7406 Germantown Avenue was used as the headmaster's house. Pennsylvania School for the Deaf moved to the former campus of Germantown Academy in 1984. (Chestnut Hill Historical Society.)

A teacher leads her class in speech lessons in 1891. Each student has a slate for writing. Vocational training, such as barbering, carpentry, welding, and shoe repair, was provided for boys and domestic arts for girls to give them a livelihood and enable them to participate fully in society. Printing was taught, and in the late 1880s, they began to publish the *Silent World*, which became the *Mount Airy World*. (Pennsylvania School for the Deaf.)

Founded in 1917 by the Sisters of St. Joseph, the Cecilian Academy (as it became known) first met at 144 West Carpenter Lane with three girls and a boy enrolled. The school expanded to five buildings with grades kindergarten through 12. Here in 1942, Cecilian students were in costume for a May Day celebration in the side yard of Elizabeth House at 138 Carpenter Lane. The high school was closed in 1990 and the lower grades in 2003. (Andrew Maginnis.)

In 1908, boys gather in the vegetable patch behind the Lutheran Orphans' Home and Asylum for the Aged, where much of the produce for the home was grown. This 1865 building survives as the Schaeffer Memorial building. Elizabeth Schaeffer established the orphanage in a rented house at 6719 Germantown Avenue in 1859. Later that year, she bought the 6950 Germantown Avenue property, shown here. The Board of Lady Managers ran it for 12 years, and then turned it over to Pennsylvania's Lutheran Ministerium. Soon elderly residents were welcomed. It provided a home for nearly 100 children who lost fathers in the Civil War. Below, "Betsy Ross and her staff" pose in 1917. The orphans attended school on campus until 1912, when they began attending public schools. No longer an orphanage, it is now the Germantown Home, a community for older citizens. (Above, Judith Callard.)

The Lutheran Theological Seminary, established in Center City Philadelphia in 1864, came to Magnolia Villa, formerly the house of James Gowen, in 1889. Here a group of students pose around 1890 in front of the newly-built dormitory, which accommodated 80 students. This facade that once faced Germantown Avenue was demolished, but the north facade remains. Much of the teaching was bilingual into the early 20th century because many students would serve German-speaking congregations in that era of extensive German immigration.

The Franklin Gowen estate rented land to the Mount Airy Country Club at the northeast corner of Gowen and Stenton Avenues, the site of the Oxford Presbyterian Church today. Founded for the residents of the Gowen Avenue area around 1892, it used this farmhouse as a clubhouse. It closed around 1910. A few blocks to the south was the Stenton Country Club, which served the newly developed Sedgwick and Stenton neighborhoods. (J. M. Duffin.)

Stapeley in Germantown (6300 Greene Street) began as a home for "aged and infirm Friends and those in sympathy with us." Founded by Anna Jeanes in 1903, her philanthropy extended to education for African Americans. She met with Booker T. Washington in 1906 and established the Negro Rural School Fund with a $1 million grant. She lived her last years at the home, dying there in 1907. This 1931 view shows the rear of Stapeley from the rose garden. (Carroll Bessey.)

Sisters Anna Leamy and Elizabeth Leamy Stout bequeathed funds for the Leamy Home for Aged and Indigent Gentlewomen, which opened in 1903 on Roumfort Road. They intended to house women of former wealth and social position, over 50 years of age, with no relatives to care for them. It survived to 1980, when it was converted to condominiums. (Chestnut Hill Historical Society.)

George Nugent was a successful Philadelphia businessman, living in Germantown, where he died in 1883. In his will, he planned for the founding of the Nugent Baptist Home on his property at 221 West Johnson Street. A home for elderly Baptist ministers and their wives, it opened in 1895. In 1909, the Nugent mansion was demolished.

In 1907, music publisher Theodore Presser founded the Presser Home for Retired Music Teachers in Center City Philadelphia. The Mount Airy building opened in 1914 beside his house on West Johnson Street. The home was designed with practice rooms for residents. Residents needed to have taught music for over 25 years, be over 65 years, and pay a $200 membership fee. At the dedication, singers were recorded on talking machine records, which were sealed in the cornerstone of the building.

The Mount Airy Football Club, shown here in 1942, played at the Allens Lane Playground. The players on this team were from the Italian American community. The playground was established by George and Gertrude Woodward in 1930. (Debbie Feldman.)

In 1953, community activists founded the Allens Lane Art Center to bring west Mount Airy residents of different races together through art, music, drama, dance, and programs such as discussion groups on racial integration. It was an outgrowth of the Henry Home and School Association. The city's first integrated summer arts camp was founded there in 1954. Sidney Poitier came to see this cast perform *A Raisin in the Sun* at the center in 1963. (Allens Lane Art Center.)

Seven

MOUNT AIRY AT HOME

The oldest part of Spring Bank, on the west side of Wissahickon Avenue between Hortter and Westview Streets, dates from the 1730s. A later owner, John Welsh, president of the Centennial Exhibition Board of Finance, donated forestland, including the Mom Rinker's Rock area to Fairmount Park. In 1883, on this promontory above the Wissahickon Creek, he placed a statue of William Penn, called *Toleration*, which he purchased at the Philadelphia Centennial Exposition.

This 1907 view looks east along Mount Airy Avenue from the corner at Chew Street. To the south of this block near Chew Street was Dunny's Pond, where local youth went swimming. Mount Airy Avenue was opened in the 1850s. The two Italianate-style houses in the foreground were built soon after.

In the 1880s, the Lloyd family played doubles tennis near Johnson Street, amid open land and pastures.

These boys are not concerned about getting wet as they catch fish in the Cresheim Creek in 1905.

Workers pause in front of the newly-built twin houses at 143, 145, 151, and 153 Carpenter Lane in 1886. Across the street is the site of the Pelham development, which was begun in 1893. (The Library Company of Philadelphia.)

Newly widened and paved Gowen Avenue, formerly Miller's Lane, looking toward Germantown Avenue, was photographed from the tower of Grace Church in 1889. In the distance are the turreted towers of the Pennsylvania School for the Deaf. The conical tops are now gone. In the center is the Mount Airy station with its stair pavilion roof on the left, now gone. A pasture is visible in the first block of Gowen Avenue off Germantown Avenue. In 1883, the Gowen family built the first houses in the new development. In 1886, coworkers William Thorne and Justus Schwacke built the twin houses in the center of the photograph, 221 and 223 East Gowen Avenue. Schwacke's son, John Strubing Schwacke, became an architect and designed his own house in the rear of the lot at 7445 Sprague Street. (Grace Epiphany Church.)

Parishioners walk home from Grace Church in front of the house at the northeast corner of East Gowen Avenue and Sprague Street (pictured in the previous photograph also). This house was used as a hospital for tuberculosis patients. Neighbors complained about the institutional use and fought it successfully all the way to the Pennsylvania Supreme Court. Things got worse for the neighbors when a builder bought the house, tore it down in 1906, and built five pairs of twin houses. (J. M. Duffin.)

Francis I. Gowen received the house at 30 East Gowen Avenue, known as "The Chimneys," as a wedding present. It was designed by Frank Furness in 1884. The Gowen family commissioned three other houses by Furness on Boyer Street for rental purposes. The Lutheran Theological Seminary bought this house in 1923 for graduate student housing and classrooms. The porch brackets and finial on the second-floor balcony roof are now gone. (Lutheran Archives Center at Philadelphia.)

Sinking a ball in the corner pocket must be tough when a snow leopard hovers in the rafters. This third-floor billiard room and its taxidermic menagerie belonged to Earl Wheeler Jenkins, who was the first owner of 334 East Gowen Avenue, designed in 1905 by Savery, Scheetz, and Savery. The house was divided into an unequal twin house, and later both sides were taken over by the De La Salle Christian brothers for living space in the 1970s. (Chestnut Hill Historical Society.)

Well-dressed children play in Carpenter's Meadow around 1915. The Fairmount Park Commission appropriated 12 acres to form Carpenter's Meadow, now Carpenter's Woods, "to preserve the watershed from contamination" in 1920 and thus blocked housing development. By then, this open space was becoming surrounded by suburban development.

In 1905, members of the McCallum family relaxed on the lawn of their home on the east side of the 6600 block Germantown Avenue. A maid brings a glass on a tray to the family, including a girl in a wheelchair with perhaps a nurse hovering over her. By this time, the family carpet mill business had been relocated from Carpenter Lane to Wayne Junction. The house no longer exists.

Morris and Sally Stout, seen here by the porch, were the first owners of 31 West Mount Pleasant Avenue, built in 1893. Their son, Morris Jr., is shown here on his toy horse with his sister, Rebecca, and her friend. Morris Sr. was one of many living in Mount Airy who, by the 1890s, commuted to work by train daily. Stout was a purchasing agent for his brother Charles's business, Evans Leather Company, in Camden, New Jersey. (David T. Moore.)

Caroline Lovett and Robert Bright were married in 1895 at Grace Church. She lived with her aunt and her adoptive mother, Charlotte Lovett Bostwick, in the "steamboat house" (see page 32). The Brights received the furnished 22 East Sedgwick Street house, below, as a wedding present from Bostwick. Here three generations pose, complete with toy horse by the fence and dog asleep in the grass. (David T. Moore.)

The Ship House (see page 20) was demolished to make way for this row of twins, built in 1907 by James J. Allen. A newspaper reported of "changing the neighborhood from farm and pasture land to pretty gardens and lawns." This photograph was used in a magazine to advertise these houses for sale or rent by Allen, who also built stores on Germantown Avenue. Pictured are 59 and 61 West Pomona Street at the corner of Cherokee Street in 1908.

In 1909, this playground was built on the site of the Pomona Grove estate on Germantown Avenue below Duval Street. Subscriptions raised improved the lot, including a 12-foot fence shielding neighbors' yards from baseballs. There, in 1910, the Pomona Tennis Club of about 30 members built a tennis court for exercise and for "the people of a newly built neighborhood to . . . promote good fellowship and a spirit of uplift in the vicinity." By 1923, storefront buildings had supplanted the playground.

William Byrd, one of the first builders in Philadelphia to build homes for fellow blacks, built 56 and 60 Good Street before 1913. In 1929, Ku Klux Klan members, resentful of his success, burned a cross on his lawn and burned part of his house at 327 East Upsal Street, then fled after being met with gun-wielding family members. Byrd maintained a realty business, which rented to blacks moving to Philadelphia from the south. (The Library Company of Philadelphia.)

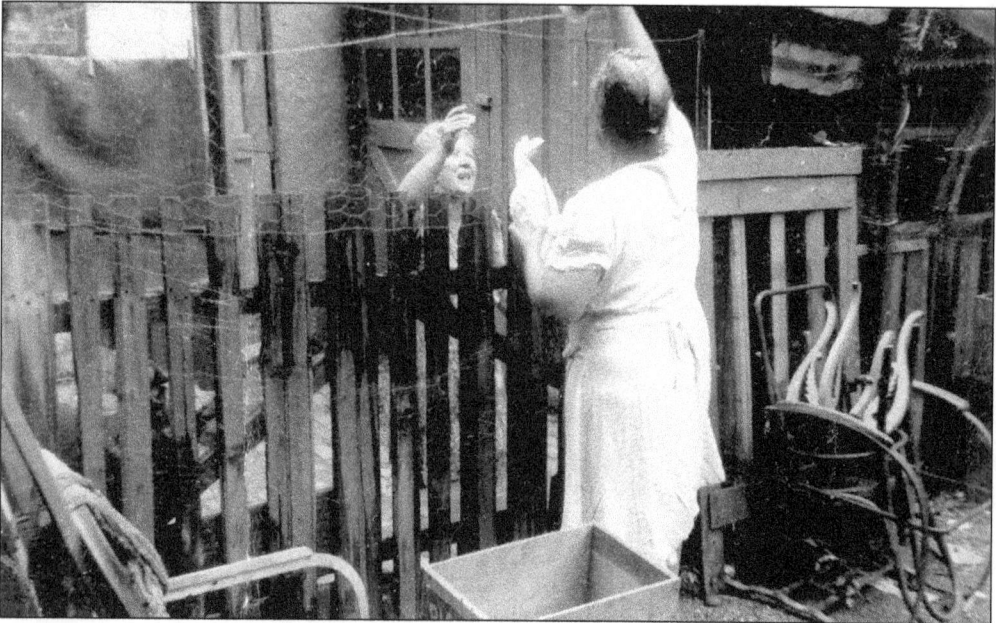

Esther Pierce Cuff (daughter of chauffeur Leander Pierce, page 65) passed containers of food back and forth over the fence at 6723 Crowson to her neighbor of German descent, Mrs. Ritchie. The Ritchies anglicized their name during World War I because of anti-German sentiment. This working-class part of east Mount Airy was a mixed race neighborhood around 1940. (Pierce/Cuff/Houston/Mack family.)

Erkie Cuff, husband of Esther, kept furniture cast off from his employers in his backyard for distribution to neighbors. Cuff was a gardener and handyman for a Jewish family, the Richmans, at 7003 Emlen Street, seen here around 1936. Harry Richman clutches his teddy bear. (Pierce/Cuff/Houston/Mack family.)

Carol Ann Hall, granddaughter of the Cuffs, sits astride a pony on Crowson Street in 1944. In the early 1940s, entrepreneurs with ponies, costumes, and cameras toured east and west Mount Airy several times a summer, earning money with portraits such as these. (Carol A. Hall Mack.)

In 1904, traffic was sparse on Lincoln Drive at Wissahickon Avenue near the site of the Rittenhouse Paper Mill dam, across the Monoshone Creek, looking toward Center City Philadelphia.

Two buildings joined by a sun porch comprised the Cresheim Arms Hotel: Dunedin to the left, built in the late 1890s, and Whitehall, designed by George Pearson in 1905. The proprietor, Laura Watson, rented rooms for the week, month, or year, furnished or unfurnished. In 1909, it was acquired by widow Rebecca Freedley. In 1913, a black author commented the hotel employed large numbers of blacks. After closing in the 1970s, the Hare Krishna sect bought it in 1977.

A surge in construction of profitable apartment buildings occurred between 1918 and 1930. The 14-story Mayfair House is seen under construction in 1926, viewed from the corner of Lincoln Drive and West Upsal Street, with 608 and 603 West Cliveden Street below. The men stand on the future site of the Cliveden Hall Apartments. The Mayfair had 209 apartments, a rooftop restaurant, a garage for residents' cars, and was a convenient ride to Center City. Nearby homeowners protested its construction. By the end of the 20th century, many apartment buildings suffered from deferred maintenance. The Mayfair was closed in 1989 and was demolished in 2000. Below, this commuter with newspaper in hand is probably walking home from the Tulpehocken station along Wayne Avenue to Lincoln Drive. A trolley car is in the distance. (Above, Free Library of Philadelphia.)

In 1910, Harold, Charles, and William Melcher moved into their new home at 616 West Hortter Street, seen here on July 4, 1911. They previously lived at 52 West Tulpehocken Street. In winter, they sometimes sledded from there to Summit Presbyterian Church. Their father, William, worked at Cramp Shipyard and was superintendent of the Sunday school. Their mother, Emma, played the organ there. William protested before their father took this photograph, "This is so fake, Father." (Sally Melcher Jarvis.)

Charles Jenkins built Far Country in 1916 at 6800 Scotforth Road. There he established the Hemlock Arboretum and bird sanctuary in 1933 and, for almost 20 years, issued the *Hemlock Bulletin*, describing plants and activities there. Jenkins installed labels for hemlocks, hollies, and other unusual plants, as well as the "Historic Walk" shown here with associative stones from around the world. In 1975, the family sold the property to Fairmount Park, which later sold the house. (Fairmount Park Commission.)

In 1902, much of east Mount Airy looked like this. The photographer was standing on Stenton Avenue, also called Township Line Road, looking east up Nolen's Lane toward Limekiln Pike, with pastures and fields as far as the eye can see.

Three girls inspect twin houses under construction between 1906 and 1911 on the 500 block of East Johnson Street before it was paved. Cliveden Park is on the right behind them. A stream runs diagonally across the park and flows into the Wingohocking Creek at Awbury Arboretum.

The Peter Hinkle farm and Charles Rittenhouse's slaughterhouse and farm extended from Germantown Avenue above Sharpnack Street to Ross Street. These older buildings, seen here in 1924, were soon to be removed as 80 new row houses were being constructed on the right, along newly opened Montana Street. Nearby East Hortter Street, below, was developed as a garden street with islands of lawn and trees, a new concept in suburban living. This view looking west from Boyer Street toward Chew Street in 1927 reveals a sign half way down on the left reading, "Sample home," and a drugstore sign at the corner. The spindly trees are now mature, and their trunks reach the curb. The stone posts in the foreground, left and right, mark alleys for cars to reach the first-floor rear garages. (Below, Philadelphia City Archives.)

Dr. George Woodward hired Robert McGoodwin in 1924 to design a master plan for a residential neighborhood in west Mount Airy called the French Village. Woodward and his wife, Gertrude, were inspired by the stone farmhouses they saw when traveling in Normandy, France. Two octagonal towers with conical roofs have stairways inside and flanking stone arches along the intersection of Allens Lane and Emlen Street. Weathervanes, a feature of many farmsteads, are included here. These commemorate Columbus's ship voyage and Lindbergh's airplane flight. Both are gone now, the latter blown away in a storm. The first purchasers of a lot (below, right) was the Joseph Priestly Button family, who downsized to this not-so-small house, 7307 Elbow Lane, designed by McGoodwin. Their son Conyers built 7311 Elbow Lane next door in 1925. (Above, Chestnut Hill Historical Society; below, Free Library of Philadelphia.)

The Tudoresque-style sales office of Ashton Tourison's Ye Sedgwick Farms Company was located at 7014 Boyer Street. It began around 1908 with "grass-bound paths and box bordered old-fashioned flowers," appealing to a suburban ideal. It was an elaborate version of the sales trailer in a new development and was eventually demolished for a new marketable home. Native son Tourison began building homes in Mount Airy in the early 1870s. (Historical Society of Pennsylvania.)

A reporter wrote in 1921, "Under the skillful management of the Tourisons the farms on the east of Germantown to Stenton Avenue . . . have become a suburb of charming villas, bungalows and mansions. The growth . . . will not stop until it has reached the Cresheim Creek." Some streets were named for celebrated Civil War Union soldiers, such as Anderson, Crittenden, and Sedgwick. Here at 614 East Sedgwick Street is an example of a neo-Georgian house, repeated at 100 East Sedgwick. (Historical Society of Pennsylvania.)

114

In 1885, Tourison opened East Sedgwick Street from Germantown Avenue to Chew Street. The first house was 32 East Sedgwick Street. He continued to construct other houses on the south side of the block. This one at 50 East Sedgwick is embellished with a tulip design. Several basic floor plans were used, but they were rearranged to create variety and individuality. Below is 514 East Sedgwick, built in 1905, photographed shortly after construction. In 1910, Frank Taylor, a West Virginia coal mine owner, and his wife bought the house. A captain in World War I, he asked the English sergeant assigned to him to return to Mount Airy as his chauffeur. The Englishman and his wife, who became the cook, lived in the garage apartment behind. Taylor's daughter's family lived in the house until 1971. (Above, Historical Society of Pennsylvania; below, Joseph Price, M.D.)

The house at 7018 Boyer Street is the backdrop for these unidentified men who may be digging a war garden as a World War I civilian initiative. Mount Airy still had undeveloped tracts such as this one into the 1920s. Because builders repeated models, the design of this house is almost identical to that of 7144 Ardleigh Street and 437 East Mount Pleasant Avenue. (J. M. Duffin.)

This "interior of the Elizabethan house, livable, luxurious and large scale" was pictured in a sales brochure for Sedgwick Farms in 1912. (Historical Society of Pennsylvania.)

In 1912, this establishment was advertised as the "Sedgwick Auto Co. fireproof garage on the premises; has every facility for the care of 25 cars." It was located along the west side of the Philadelphia and Reading Railroad tracks on Sprague Street between Gorgas Lane and Sedgwick Street. Later a riding stable occupied this site. (Historical Society of Pennsylvania.)

61 Trains Daily to STENTON. 9¢ FARE   **STENTON**   ———ALL——— CITY IMPROVEMENTS

Chestnut Hill Branch READING RAILWAY   Station on property—24 Minutes to Terminal

| Write for Book of Photographs showing various Types of Houses. | **FRANK MAURAN** 239 LAND TITLE BUILDING |

Frank Mauran developed an area called Stenton, shown here at the intersection of Ardleigh Street and Vernon Road around 1909. For the recreation of the new suburbanites, there was the Stenton Country Club at the northeast corner of Vernon Road and Stenton Avenue. (Historical Society of Pennsylvania.)

During World War II, Louis Stevens allowed neighbors to plant a victory garden along the 400 block of West Mount Airy Avenue. After the war ended, Tot Lot was born here. This child-care cooperative was marked by the sense of community for which Mount Airy is known. Around 1960, Dena Dannenberg gives a child a push on a swing. While forming friendships, parents arranged schedules, clean-up crews, and craft projects and constructed playground equipment. Tot Lot continues today. (Dena Dannenberg.)

C. DeLores Tucker, who lived at 6700 Lincoln Drive for 47 years, worked for decades in the civil rights movement, marching in Selma, Alabama, with Rev. Dr. Martin Luther King Jr. in 1965. Tucker, seen here at a voting rally in 1971, was Pennsylvania's secretary of state, the first African American in the United States to hold this office. She effectively crusaded for women's rights and the welfare of children. (African American Museum in Philadelphia.)

Eight

PELHAM

In 1893, one hundred acres of the Carpenter estate, Phil-Ellena, was deeded to a syndicate formed to develop Pelham. Carpenter Lane, Germantown Avenue, Hortter Street, and the Chestnut Hill West Railroad line largely formed Pelham's borders. The Carpenter Land and Improvement Company, financed by Anthony J. Drexel and Edward Stotesbury, hired Herman Wendell and Willard Smith as Pelham's managers and developers. Wendell and Smith had worked on other developments in Wayne and Overbrook. Their office was here at 515 Pelham Road (now a dwelling), with the steam plant behind on Hortter Street. (Historical Society of Pennsylvania.)

The new planned suburban community had wide, curving streets with sidewalks, brick gutters, and sewers. The company set minimum prices for houses and required setbacks from the street. Pelham may have gotten its name from a best-selling book at the time, Lord Lytton's tale of adventure. From the future site of the Emlen Arms on newly laid out Emlen Street, this photograph was taken facing southeast and shows Pelham Road intersecting at the dip in the road. In the far distance is an 1830s house that predates the development, now 166 West Hortter Street. The photograph below shows the front fence of this house (on the right), looking toward Germantown Avenue along Hortter Street, then called Franklin Street. Emlen Street is in the foreground, with a newly installed lamppost and fire hydrant. (Lois Frischling.)

The company also owned land on the other side of Lincoln Avenue (now Drive), but there sold lots rather than designed houses. This new boulevard cut a swath through Mount Airy, ending at Carpenter Street (now Lane), one block up from this view, seen in 1895. Looking northwest away from Pelham, McCallum Street (on the left) crosses Lincoln Avenue. Next is a large Queen Anne–style twin, still there today at 441 and 443 Carpenter Lane. (Historical Society of Pennsylvania.)

This photograph shows the intersection of Pelham and Hortter Streets. The empty lot in the foreground is the site of 375 Pelham Road, built around 1912. Part of the development's success stemmed from the proximity of the Carpenter and Upsal train stations, making commuting to central Philadelphia convenient. The railroad siding branching off the main track to the left brought coal to the steam plant, which heated Pelham's homes until the 1960s. Underground pipes melted snow in the streets.

Architect-designed houses began to go up in Pelham from 1893 into the early 20th century. The variety of architectural styles, with pricing for different income levels, contributed to the success of the community of over 300 houses. Attention to design was not just reserved for mansions. Twin houses at 131 and 133 West Phil-Ellena Street, designed by Keen and Mead in 1894, were in "Spanish Style" according to the 1896 *Scientific American, Building Edition.* (Historical Society of Pennsylvania.)

The terra-cotta medallion above the third floor of this lavish twin house at 580 Pelham Road records the date 1894 in curvilinear numerals, flanked by cherubs, one blowing a trumpet. They seem to announce to people disembarking from the Upsal station that they have arrived in Pelham. A for sale sign is on the lawn. In 1949, this house became the St. Madeleine Sophie Convent, and in 1984, it became the Interim House. (Historical Society of Pennsylvania.)

The families moving into Pelham were not part of the old Philadelphia social elite but rather were successful members of the mercantile class. The houses were built for large families with live-in servants. Pictured shortly after it was built in 1895, 140 West Phil-Ellena Street was designed by architect William L. Price.

Houses were carefully sited to preserve trees from the Carpenter estate, Phil-Ellena. The Pelham School, at 539 Pelham Road, was built as a private home and became Miss Norris' Boarding and Day School in 1907. Bertha and Mary Norris, Bryn Mawr graduates, employed an all-female, college-educated faculty to teach academic subjects, languages, art, and sewing to children in kindergarten through high school. College preparation was provided. Boys were admitted through third grade. (Lois Frischling.)

A brochure for the development described the Pelham kitchen as "a gem. It is a servant keeper." This kitchen light fixture combined a downward-facing electric bulb with a gas uplight. All Pelham houses had electricity, gas, indoor plumbing, and heat from the central steam plant, the latest technology.

Pelham Court apartments at 6809 Emlen Street were advertised as one minute from Carpenter station, adjoining the Automobile Club of Germantown and between the Germantown and Philadelphia Cricket Clubs. Apartment buildings were not included in Pelham's development plan, and commercial properties were restricted to Germantown Avenue. In Mount Airy, large homes sometimes gave way to apartment buildings. This building was constructed after 1906 on Alice Molten's former property. By 1911, her house was replaced by a mirror image of this building.

In 1909, the Pelham Trust Company erected this building, designed by Thomas and Churchman, at 6740 Germantown Avenue. In 1911, the basement was renovated as storage vaults for silverware and jewelry and leased to Pelham residents in response to recent robberies in Mount Airy and Chestnut Hill. The company provided pick-up and delivery service. In 1927, it merged with Germantown Trust Company.

When the Automobile Club of Germantown was built in 1894, fewer than 500 cars were registered in all of Philadelphia. Although a full-time mechanic was employed at the club, about half of the more than 55 members did not own cars. The club functioned as a social club where members could dine, bowl, and play billiards, cards, or tennis. A parlor was maintained for women, and a ballroom was added to the south side after this photograph was taken. Today it is the Commodore Barry Club.

INDEX

Visit us at
arcadiapublishing.com